Muinji'j Asks Why

The Story of the Mi'kmaq and the Shubenacadie Residential School

Told by **MUINJI'J** & **SHANIKA MACEACHERN**

Illustrated by **ZETA PAUL**

NIMBUS
PUBLISHING LTD.
——— NIMBUS.CA ———

Information found in this book may be difficult for some readers. Learning about the realities of Indian Residential Schools can bring forward many emotions for survivors, their ancestors, and for other readers who have experienced trauma in their own lives. We respectfully ask that you be aware of this as you read, or read to others. For those in need of help, the Indian Residential Schools Crisis Line, reachable at 1-800-721-0066, is available 24 hours a day.

One day, Muinji'j came home from school very upset. Her grandparents could tell right away by her sad eyes and her heavy shoulders.

"Muinji'j, what has made you so sad?" they asked.

"Nana, Papa, today at school our teacher talked to us about residential schools."

Her grandparents gave each other a look, like they knew just what she would say.

"Everyone was talking about residential schools because of what was in the news, the story about the children," Muinji'j continued. "The teacher told us different things than what you have told us. I tried to tell her what you said and she wouldn't let me."

Nana wrapped Muinji'j in a hug. It was soft but hard at the same time. "The story of the Mi'kmaw people is one that very few truly know, Ladybug. Even fewer understand what happened at the residential schools. It is a hard story to tell, but you must know the truth.

"Sit and I will tell you the story."

A long time ago, this place they call Nova Scotia had one people, the Mi'kmaq. They were beautiful people with long silky black hair, sun-kissed brown skin, and deep brown eyes, just like you. And they loved this land, Mi'kma'ki.

They lived differently than people do today. Everything they had came from Mother Earth. They built their homes, called wigwams, and the canoes in which they travelled from the trees, and they wore clothes made from the animals they hunted for food.

Our people respected all of nature. They only took what was needed and wasted nothing, leaving dried tobacco on the land in thanks for Mother Earth's gifts.

Children were loved and cherished by all in Mi'kma'ki. Everyone knew the little ones would be the knowledge keepers for generations to come.

Children learned from their Elders through stories. These stories helped the children understand the world they lived in, and the world that had come before.

They taught them that their long braids held the teachings of their people and that they would give them strength.

They taught them that the people who live today are connected to the people who came before. They taught them to protect the land and the water for the people who would come after them.

They taught them all they needed to know.

Then one day, other people came.

They looked different and sounded different. Their skin was pale and their words were sharp. Still, the Mi'kmaq welcomed them, and helped them explore Mi'kma'ki. They traded and celebrated together and made promises to each other to share the land. They called these promises treaties.

But as time passed, the Mi'kmaq learned that these other people not only looked and sounded different, but they thought differently, too. They had begun to see these lands as their own.

They had forgotten their promises to the Mi'kmaq.

They had forgotten we had taught them the ways of the land.

They had forgotten the old name, Mi'kma'ki, and so they called this place Nova Scotia.

As more time passed, the other people carved the land into smaller and smaller pieces. Nova Scotia became part of a new country called Canada, and our people faded into the background.

The people who made the rules in Canada thought their way was the only way.

They wanted everyone to dress the same,

talk the same,

and think the same.

To be Canadian was to be like them.

But there was a problem.

The Mi'kmaw people did not

think,

talk,

or look like them.

The men who made all the rules were stubborn in their beliefs, and they tried to change the Mi'kmaq. They made our people live in small communities called reservations rather than off the land as they always had.

Our people were separated from one another and no longer able to live in our traditional ways.

Though the people of Canada had taken the land, they knew the Mi'kmaq still held their own beliefs. The men with all the power told the Mi'kmaq their beliefs were wrong and that if they didn't change, our people would not go to heaven. This sounded really scary to the Mi'kmaq.

The men with all the power told our people to stop speaking Mi'kmaq, and to speak English or French instead.

But the Mi'kmaq did not change.

The men who had all the power started to get angry.

They told the Mi'kmaq they couldn't leave their communities. They would go to jail if they did.

They told the Mi'kmaq they could not practice their traditions. They would go to jail if they did.

They told the Mi'kmaq they could not have large gatherings. They would go to jail if they did.

The Mi'kmaw people were scared, and sad, and missed their old ways of life.

But still they did not change.

They still spoke Mi'kmaq.

They still believed in what they had always believed.

And they still dressed as they had always dressed.

The men with all the power became angrier. They made more laws and more rules, trying to make everyone the same.

But still, it did not work.

Then one day, the men with all the power had an idea.

A terrible idea.

What if we teach all the children to be the same?

What if we build schools and teach the children our ways and help them forget their ways?

We can teach them to speak our way, dress our way, think our way.

"Yes!" said the men who had all the power.

So they started to build.

CANADA

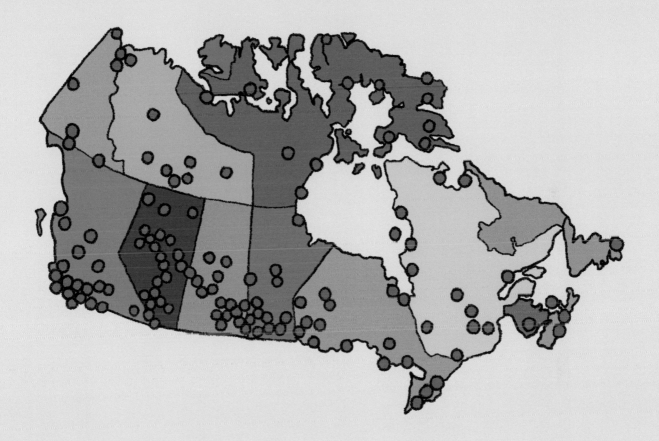

They started to build schools.

Small schools, medium schools, and large schools. They built schools in the east and schools in the west; they built schools in the north and schools in the south—and everywhere in between.

They decided that every Indigenous child must go.
They all needed to be taught the Canadian way of life.

The men with all the power sent their police to our communities to gather our children.

One by one, they were all gathered up: 150,000 children in all.

No child could be left behind. This was the law, and they all had to go.

Parents were scared for their children. They cried, begged, and pleaded to keep their children home, but it was the law. So when the police came for the children, the moms and dads told their children they loved them, told them to be strong, and to do as they were told.

The children were taken.

Our children were taken.

In Nova Scotia, our children were sent to a place called the Shubenacadie Residential School.

It was a large brick building on a hill overlooking the Shubenacadie River. Children from all over Mi'kma'ki—what they called Nova Scotia, New Brunswick, and Prince Edward Island—were brought there. Hundreds of children, some as young as three.

"Papa, I wouldn't have let them take me," said Muinji'j.
"I would have run into the woods to hide."

"Some children did hide, Tu's, but you couldn't hide forever.
They would find you at your home, at your friend's house, or
even at your nana's if you tried to hide. Some communities were
spared, but most children had to go."

These schools were not at all like schools today. They were not safe or welcoming. The schools were run by the churches, not by teachers and principals. Shubenacadie was a Catholic residential school, which meant they had priests and nuns for teachers.

The teachers did not see Mi'kmaw children as beautiful and kind like they do today.

When the children first arrived, the nuns went straight to work making the children look alike.

They cut their long black hair. They threw away their old clothing and made them wear uniforms.

This was the proper way to look, they told them: the Canadian way. Their old clothes were wrong. Their hair was messy and dirty. And their braids did not hold the strength and wisdom of their ancestors.

Most children who went to residential schools lived there all year long, sometimes for many years if their communities were far away. Some never saw their parents, or their home, again.

Life at these schools was hard,

it was scary,

and it was lonely.

When the children tried to speak their language, the nuns and priests would punish them. They were only to speak English at the Shubenacadie Residential School. They learned quickly to obey the teachers and to only speak English.

When none of the nuns or priests were listening, they would whisper in their own language to each other to try to remember.

"Wait, what language were they speaking, Papa? Everyone here speaks English. Except for Kiju, great-grandmother, but I can never understand what she's saying."

"That's because she speaks Mi'kmaq, Tu's."

"Mi'kmaq is the name of our people but it is also the name of our language," Papa explained. "One of the things the residential schools stole from us was our language. Before them, all of our people spoke Mi'kmaq. Today, only a few can speak it. Without knowing our language, we have lost part of our culture and identity. Someday I hope that all Mi'kmaw children, like you, will learn our language at school."

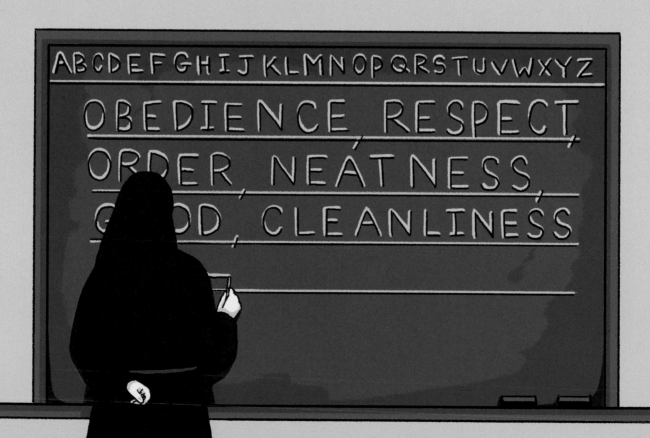

"I want to learn Mi'kmaq, Papa. Why don't I know Mi'kmaq? You have to teach me."

"I only know a few words, Tu's. I need to learn Mi'kmaq just like you, but here is an important word I know: *L'nu*. It means 'the people,' which is what we call ourselves.

"And another important word is *kitpu*, it means eagle. Eagles are sacred to our people: they fly the highest in the sky and are the closest to the Creator."

Muinji'j's eyes were wide. There was so much to learn. "What happened next to *L'nu*, Papa?"

"As time passed, the children started to believe the Mi'kmaw ways were wrong. That their traditions were something to be ashamed of, that the eagle was just an animal, and that their language should not be spoken. This was all they knew at the Shubenacadie Residential School.

They started to think differently.

They started to think the same.

Year after year, for thirty-seven long years, children were brought to the Shubenacadie Residential School. Only when the children turned sixteen were they told to return to their communities. But when the children did finally return home, they were confused.

They could still see the beauty of Mi'kma'ki, but they were afraid to be proud. They had been taught to be ashamed of their people, their community. They were afraid they would be punished for wanting to be Mi'kmaq. But they were also afraid to be Canadian.

Where did they fit?

They were not like the Mi'kmaq who had not gone to the residential school, and they were not like other Canadians.

They had been taught at the schools that they would fit in with society now, but they didn't seem to fit anywhere.

For years, the people of Canada did not believe us when we told them how terrible the schools were. They did not listen. They did not stop the harm. Some of those schools would not close for a long time.

Finally, after hundreds of years, the men with all the power realized the harm they had caused. The terrible Shubenacadie School closed for good in 1967, and our people started to heal.

To heal from the hurt.

To heal from the shame.

To heal from all of the things that were taken away.

Muinji'j felt many emotions. She was sad for her people, and angry that they had lost so much. But she still had one big question that hadn't been answered.

"Papa, you didn't tell me about why children died there. My teacher said that children were buried at residential schools. Is that true?"

Papa had tears in his eyes, and he took Muinji'j's hand in his. "One of the saddest things about the residential schools was that not all of the children who went there made it back home.

"When the schools first opened, there were lots of sicknesses the people who ran the schools didn't know how to cure. These sicknesses caused many children to die.

"They also did many unkind things to the children which caused them to become sick, and some children did not heal."

"What happened to them?" asked Muinji'j. "Didn't parents come for their children when they were sick?"

Papa shook his head. "The schools would not allow the parents to come. Most times, the parents would not know their child was sick until it was too late. Some did not even know that their child had died until the summer came and their son or daughter didn't return home.

"I know this part of the story is really hard, Muinji'j," said Papa. "It is hard to imagine a child dying at school. The truth is, children did die at the residential schools, and some were buried on the schoolground without proper acknowledgment, like a gravestone. Some returned home, but many did not."

"But after the schools were closed and the children came home, everyone was okay—right, Nana?"

Nana gave Muinji'j a sad smile she knew well. "I wish I could say that was true, Ladybug. But our communities still suffer today because of those schools and the terrible things that happened there. It is hard to heal from suffering that lasts lifetimes. It is hard to heal when so much was taken away and so much harm was done. But our people work together to heal and to be well. It is time now for all of Canada to help us heal."

"Well, they can't hurt me!"

"You are right, Muinji'j; those schools are all closed now. No one will ever have to go to a residential school again."

"Are you sure I will never have to go to a residential school?"

"Yes," said Nana. "Because of the suffering of our people, no one will ever have to go to a residential school again.

Today we live by Etuapmumk, what we call "two-eyed seeing": one eye for the Mi'kmaw ways and one for the Canadian ways. We as Ľnu understand the Canadian ways and accept them as part of our lives, but we also hold strong to our traditions and culture."

Muinji'j had learned a lot about her people and their history, but still had one question left. Maybe the most important question of all.

"Papa, how will we make sure our teachers know our story, the true story?"

"We will tell them," said Papa.

"How?"

"We just did."

Nimbus Publishing Limited

3660 Strawberry Hill Street, Halifax, NS, B3K 5A9

(902) 455-4286 nimbus.ca

Printed and bound in Canada

Design: Heather Bryan

Editor: Whitney Moran

NB1621

This story was made possible in part due to the support of Valley Credit Union. Valley Credit Union recognizes that Truth and Reconciliation is the responsibility of all Canadians.

The authors wish to extend sincere gratitude to Marilyn Perkins of Glooscap First Nation. Her wise guidance was greatly appreciated.

Library and Archives Canada Cataloguing in Publication

Title: Muinji'j asks why : the story of the Mi'kmaq and the Shubenacadie Residential School / told by Muinji'j & Shanika MacEachern ; illustrated by Zeta Paul.

Names: MacEachern, Muinji'j, author | MacEachern, Shanika, author. | Paul, Zeta, illustrator.

Identifiers: Canadiana (print) 20210354364 | Canadiana (ebook) 20210354429 ISBN 9781774710470 (hardcover) | ISBN 9781774710500 (EPUB)

Subjects: LCSH: Shubenacadie Indian Residential School (Shubenacadie, N.S.)—Juvenile literature. | CSH: First Nations—Nova Scotia—Residential schools—Juvenile literature. | CSH: First Nations children—Nova Scotia—Social conditions—20th century—Juvenile literature. | CSH: First Nations children—Violence against—Nova Scotia—History—20th century—Juvenile literature.

Classification: LCC E96.6.S58 M33 2021 | DDC j371.829/97071635—dc23

Nimbus Publishing acknowledges the financial support for its publishing activities from the Government of Canada, the Canada Council for the Arts, and from the Province of Nova Scotia. We are pleased to work in partnership with the Province of Nova Scotia to develop and promote our creative industries for the benefit of all Nova Scotians.